Melissa Grönebaum

Kant's radical evil. Religion within the boundary of pure reason

GRIN Verlag

Bibliografische Information der Deutschen Nationalbibliothek:

Die Deutsche Bibliothek verzeichnet diese Publikation in der Deutschen National-
bibliografie; detaillierte bibliografische Daten sind im Internet über http://dnb.d-
nb.de/ abrufbar.

Imprint:

Copyright © 2013 GRIN Verlag GmbH
Druck und Bindung: Books on Demand GmbH, Norderstedt Germany
ISBN: 978-3-656-58671-5

This book at GRIN:

http://www.grin.com/en/e-book/268385/kant-s-radical-evil-religion-within-the-
boundary-of-pure-reason

GRIN - Your knowledge has value

Der GRIN Verlag publiziert seit 1998 wissenschaftliche Arbeiten von Studenten, Hochschullehrern und anderen Akademikern als eBook und gedrucktes Buch. Die Verlagswebsite www.grin.com ist die ideale Plattform zur Veröffentlichung von Hausarbeiten, Abschlussarbeiten, wissenschaftlichen Aufsätzen, Dissertationen und Fachbüchern.

NAME: Melissa Groenebaum

ESSAY TITLE: Kant's radical evil

WORD COUNT AND PAGE LENGTH OF ESSAY: 2127 words 3 pages

1. In what sense or senses is Evil radical for Kant?

„Der Mensch ist von Natur aus böse." (Human nature is evil) Stating this, Kant refers to a problem which has been from time immemorial a problem of Moral Philosophy. But what exactly does Kant mean, stating this? One interpretation could be that nature brings the evilness from the outside and makes a human evil, that it is the environment which is responsible for any human evilness. Another interpretation could be that men are evil by nature in a way that they are born evil and evilness is a human's feature, why everybody is evil. Probably Kant did not either mean the one nor the other. To a greater degree, Kant assumes that there is an evil propensity (*Hang zum Bösen*) in everyone from the beginning on, which men can fall for. As written in the bible's first book of Moses, the prehistoric men, who are meant to be Adam and Eve and serve as an orientation for Kant, were, living in the Garden of Eden, absolutely innocent until evil, represented by a snake, seduced them. As punishment for breaking God's Law and sinning, God expelled Adam and Eve from paradise. This first fall for evil is known as original sin. Using this example, Kant explains that the human essence is good but gets spoiled. But if human beings are essentially good, why does Kant state that human nature is radically evil? And what exactly does the term evil describe anyway? God's law, no matter in which religion, or the constitution decide what is right and what is wrong, therefore also which acting can be regarded as good and which as evil. Acting against any law will be punished and the counteracting person will be seen as being evil. That is, what already children are taught. The question now is what criteria one has to fulfill to be rightfully esteemed as being evil. But it is not enough to simply regard the acting. Crucial is the condition of maxim. The motive why an action is done makes it good or evil. Consequently, just looking at the action cannot be the criteria for a good or evil categorization of a human. Human nature, which Kant is talking about, does not only describe acting but also one's motives for acting in a certain way. Terms such as sensuality, freedom, and reason must not be disregarded while analyzing the question of good and evil concerning human nature, since a human as a free being should be able to reasonable decide to regard or disregard the moral law. Regarding the case of Adam and Eve, humans seem to have to make their own decision although evil seems to be somehow included in human nature and also appears very powerful, since it, at least in this case, conquers good. The even most interesting question then, however, is, in what sense or senses evil is radical for Kant.

In the beginning, everyone is good, since in every human there is a good pre-disposition (*Anlage zum Guten*). As long as there is no freedom, the human being is innocent. However, as soon as there is a choice of acting good or evil, the human's (natural) evil propensity appears and follows the evil driving force, which leads the human to act against the moral law. This so called '*Hang zum Bösen*', is, assumed by Kant, the subjective reason of the possibility of penchant, the desire for pleasure, which becomes obvious in the case of any intoxicating medium. „Aller Hang ist entweder physisch (…) oder moralisch“[1] (every propensity is either physical or moral), which means that it either belongs to power of choice as natural being, in which case there could not be any propensity, since there has to be a freedom of the power of choice, which is not given under the circumstances of a state of nature, in which instincts and sensuality are dominant, or as moral being. There is a subjective determinant of the power of choice, which forgoes every action. („ein subjektiver Bestimmungsgrund der Willkür, der vor jeder Tat vorhergeht“[2]). There is no pre-disposition for evil, as it is the case for good. Even if the *Hang* was inherent, it would still be adopt by the men's power of choice. The origin of evil has to be freedom. But what is evil? If one looks up the term evil which is '*böse*' in German, what one should keep in mind since Kant was German, one will find several different meanings. For example, evil can be referred to immoral acting, or describe rude behavior. Additionally, evil describes anything unpleasant such as an evil smell. Kant, however, starts from the premise of morality. His categorization of evil will be elaborated. In general Kant does not assume that human beings are completely fallen for evil and therefore goes into the matter of evil in human nature. Becoming evil or letting evil taking control means to adopt evil and to except evil coming from the outside and exerting power. Consequently, it is a decision which is made by every single person, being aware of this decision and led by any driving forces. Kant stresses that this could be observed regarding any indigenous people as well as regarding any civilized people, in both each individual life and collective lives. The decision of adopting a maxim which super ordinates non-moral interests of moral interests, because of any driving forces, appears to be a basic characteristic of human nature, a natural propensity (*natürlicher Hang*) of human beings. The freedom of choice's ability or disability to absorb the moral law into one's maxim could be, according to Kant, described as a good or evil heart. Elaborating this statement, Kant defines three steps. The first step was the weakness of the human heart. The person might have had something good in mind, but failed to complete the good action. In this case the driving forces

---

[1] Kant, S.37
[2] Kant, S.38

were to strong and the human's heart to weak. The second step would be the propensity to mix immoral driving forces with moral ones, which could be also possible if one's motives are good. Kant calls this condition ‚*Unlauterkeit*' (disingenuousness). The third step is described by Kant as being the propensity of adopting evil maxims, which was the pure evilness of a human being. Mentioned evilness strikes the roots in the human's disposition and perforates all basics of the human's maxims and the human heart gets debauched. Consequently, humans can either be evil or good, nether both at the same time. Evil is depending on maxims, which organizes the importance of the driving forces and gives them more or less power. Therefore the maxims are responsible for every action, while humans tend to fall for evil maxims. Evil is nothing which is has a biological origin in human nature, but can still be found in every human. Evil is something which is likely to be adopted by men, since the *Hang* (propensity) is inherent and can be seen as some kind of illness or defect. This is why evil is somehow inherent but still acquired by free will. But in which sense is evil radical? Because of the interweaving of evil with freedom and humanity, Kant regards evil as a radical inherent but self-imposed evil of human nature men are not just by nature but radical evil. Adopting a illegal maxim is radical evil since this means to ruin all kind of one's moral principles from the ground up. A human being in general was not necessarily evil all through, but radical evil, in any case, which was also shown by experience. But where does this radical evil come from? The reason of evil, cannot, assumed by Kant, lay in sensuality, which one cannot and should not be allowed to make responsible. On the contrary, the '*Hang zum Bösen*' (propensity of evil) should be taken into consideration, which inheres man, who is understood as a free acting being, and could be found by nature. The more the human culture develops (which could nowadays be observed very well), the more guilty pleasures are brought up, for example: rapacity, envy, jealousy and accompanying the resulting actions such as lying, stingy, greed, and gloating. However, humans are never accidentally led to evil. To add, it is not the moral law giving reason, which just turns from good to evil. It always is the human him- or herself who decides to turn his or her back on the moral law. Men, as free acting beings, are aware of giving evil first choice and placing immoral maxims over the moral law. But naming malicious reason – instead of sensuality- as the cause of morally evilness in human nature on the other hand would be too much. Evil is not made by sensuality, since this would let a human being appear beastly but it is not made by reason, also, since in this case a human being would appear diabolic. Thus, evil has to come from the choice of freedom. Each human is guilty of his or her own evilness. That is why Kant calls the evil radical. It conquers the human cast of mind and from the beginning on it hinders the good germ, which is somewhere in every human, to spread. But however the evil is created, what its features are or where it comes from, in any case it can be assumed that there is no biological cause for evil and that it is not passed on by heredity; therefore it has nothing to do, stated by Kant, with something like a original sin, congenital disease or hereditary guilt, how the medical, juristically or theological faculties might call it, even though each human individual is affected by evil. In fact, a human being first is innocent and then somehow becomes evil. Every human action is free and therefore has to be judged as an originally usage of the freedom of choice. Nothing all the world over could change the fact that a human being is a free acting being. Evil has to have his origin in the human's reason. Evil does not result from a lack of moral law or the disability to act correlating to the moral law but only from the conscious decision against the moral law and therefore results from freedom. Stating this, Kant in a way stresses that the origin of evil is as indefinable as the origin of a human's freedom. Since evil is inherent and radical, the only way to overcome evil is not only a improvement of morals, or a disciplining of the nature of undisciplined propensities, but to a greater degree a revolution of one's cast of mind. The restoration of good can only take place if one manages the difficulties of turning the evil maxim into good a maxim, which requires a change of mind. Kant lets to be known that being a lawfully good person was not difficult But a lawfully good acting person, however, could still be evil. Crucial is the condition of maxim. The motive why an action is done makes it good or evil. Consequently, only that person, who possesses a good maxim, can be regarded as being good. An evil person could accidently act in a good way, or even on purpose, but the maxim then will still be evil (e.g vices of culture.). Undoubted, one must not define a person as good or evil, just because of his or her actions. Being good or evil cannot be defined by experience from the outside; it is about good maxims inside of a person and cannot be seen. The one and only good maxim is duty. But becoming a morally good person means to overcome the radical evil, which is supposed by Kant to be challenging. It requests a lot of effort and is only possible because every human also owns, besides the evil propensity, the above mentioned good pre-disposition which enables the willing human being to overcome the radical evil, with the help of a likewise willing fellowship, and to become a morally good human being. All in all, evil is in so far radical for Kant, since he claims that every human has an evil propensity (*Hang zum Bösen*) which is, since it always has to be self-imposed, to be regarded as a radical, inherent evil of human nature which is why every human being is necessarily radical evil, even though a human being is innocent in the beginning. Evil then is formed when one decides to freely adopt a evil maxim because of any driving forces and place it over the moral law, and since it perforates all basics of the human's maxims, Kant assumes it to be radical.

Source:

Kant, Immanuel (1794): Die Religion innerhalb der Grenzen der bloßen Vernunft. Felix Meiner Verlag.